HOPE
&
JOY

A Book of Hope and A Book of Joy

RONALD HARVEY WOHL

Inspiring Voices books may be ordered through booksellers or by contacting:

Inspiring Voices
1663 Liberty Drive
Bloomington, IN 47403
www.inspiringvoices.com
1-(866) 697-5313

Cover Illustration by Anabelle Lombard

Because of the dynamic nature of the Internet, any web addresses or
links contained in this book may have changed since publication and
may no longer be valid. The views expressed in this work are solely those
of the author and do not necessarily reflect the views of the publisher,
and the publisher hereby disclaims any responsibility for them.

ISBN: 978-1-4624-0656-2 (sc)
ISBN: 978-1-4624-0655-5 (e)

Library of Congress Control Number: 2013909958

Printed in the United States of America.

Inspiring Voices rev. date: 04/14/2014

Contents

A Book of Joy

Dedication

This book of poetry resulted from a challenge put to me by my wife, Myrna, of over 48 years and my best friend for the past 53 years. I have been writing poetry since my father passed away when I was 12 years old. I chose this form because it gives me quicker access to my heart and soul. Sharing those feelings with others is my best therapy and I advise you, dear reader, to do the same. For her love, grace, brilliance and companionship, I dedicate this book to my wife, *Washington, DC, 2014.*

Acknowledgement

It's not easy creating a book of poetry. There are a lot of people who have helped me along the way. I am especially grateful to all who have read or listened to my poems over the years and who have encouraged me to publish this book. My special thanks goes to Joyce Smith, who helped me with her reading, editing and friendship.

Preface

Each poem is an intimate expression that may **cause you to connect with a feeling or emotion of your own.** I hope that the feelings with which you identify will help you deal with life strongly, but sweetly.

Each poem is written on a facing page opposite a blank page on which you can write, create, illustrate or paste-in something that the poem means to you. Then, if you wish, you can scan and upload your feelings to this poem's web page at www.Hope-and-Joy.com to share with me and others.

To My Readers

Hope is a feeling
grown by the seed
of a reader's sigh
planted in shallow beds,
watered with random tears,
and warmed by the
fond remembrance of a smile.
Hope is this author's thought
that you will enjoy the visions
my words and dreams bring to mind.

A
BOOK
of
HOPE

Hope is Growing

Please write or illustrate below what this poem means to you.

Share your insights with our community by posting them to this poem's web page at www.Hope-and-Joy.com

Hope is Growing

Hope is growing
in a tiny spot
near an oak tree
on my mountain lot.
Where squirrels climb
on redbud
and dogwood trees
and leave acorns
to grow in dark, rich loam,
under fall strewn leaves.

Weathering silently
through winter's endless frost.
Hope rests uneasy
beneath granite rock,
but even with
such saddened start,
Hope grows.

From a tiny seed,
buried cold
and damp,
beneath dark
grey clouds
of sorrow
and lost beginnings,
Hope still stirs—
nurtured only
by sunless rain
and quiet snow.

But, with time,
Hope grows—
via sun-warmed springs
and summer heat,
to displace the doubt
from winter's frozen sheet.

Hope is The Essence of God

Please write or illustrate below what this poem means to you.

Share your insights with our community by posting them to this poem's web page at ***www.Hope-and-Joy.com***

Hope is The Essence of God

Hope is the essence of God.
A belief greater than just in yourself
or in anyone you could come to know.
Hope is the belief that the cosmic plan
will see your fulfillment someday,
in some way,
whether riches
are measured in gold
or in smiles,
in your pocket
or just
your heart.

Hope is the reincarnation of love,
The joy of a better tomorrow,
the cure for an unknown sickness,
the food to nurture a starving baby
or an absent mind,
the beginning of joy,
and the end of pain.

Hope is a Locket

Please write or illustrate below what this poem means to you.

Share your insights with our community by posting them to this poem's web page at ***www.Hope-and-Joy.com***

Hope is A Locket

Hope is a locket
containing a picture of a loved one,
a memento of a moment shared in love,
or a mirror to see what God
is capable of creating.

Hope is God's secret language
to decipher God's thoughts
and accomplish deeds
that bring harmony
to a difficult world…
generation after generation,
prayer after prayer.

The power of God
is the power of hope.

Hope is The Spray

Please write or illustrate below what this poem means to you.

*Share your insights with our community by posting them to this poem's web page at **www.Hope-and-Joy.com***

Hope is The Spray

Hope is the spray
of stain remover
splashed on too long-dried
food spots on a favorite blouse.

Hope is dousing
red spaghetti splatters
with milk and enzymes
after a business dinner with the boss
to discuss your future,
after a mission's loss.

Hope is seeing last night's dinner
safely down the washbasin drain,
away from silky whites and fine knits.

Hope is flapping,
wrinkled wash,
hung to dry
on a makeshift line,
ironed just in time
for wearing at this morning's
meeting with the boss
to discuss your new assignment
and your unstained record.

Hope is A Pink Carnation

Please write or illustrate below what this poem means to you.

Share your insights with our community by posting them to this poem's web page at **www.Hope-and-Joy.com**

Hope is A Pink Carnation

Hope is a pink carnation
on a high school senior's tuxedo jacket,
all dressed up in his first store rented outfit
as he waits at his date's front door;
sweat dripping down his sides
and the back of his neck—
from his fresh shorn flat top
and a reaction to his dad's
aftershave and deodorant—
a costly purple orchid corsage
in the plastic container
in his left hand,
as he rings the bell
and then remembers
his date said she would be wearing
a Kelly green prom dress.

Hope is the light
in his date's eyes
as she opens the door
and sees the most handsome
member of the Prom King's Court,
with just the right color corsage
—no matter what color it is.

Hope is A Beat Up Pick-up Truck

Please write or illustrate below what this poem means to you.

Share your insights with our community by posting them to this poem's web page at www.Hope-and-Joy.com

Hope is A Beat Up Pick-up Truck

Hope is a beat up pick-up truck
—a hundred years old—
sitting in tall weeds
on a vacant farm lot
in West Virginia,
while a slow-eyed schoolboy
counts out his hard earned cash
into the calloused hands
of an old farmer
glad to be rid of it
and satisfied
he received enough
money for propane
to keep his tin-roofed house
warm during
the cruel mountain winter ahead.

Just as satisfied that each made a good deal,
they load the junker
onto the boy's uncle's flat bed truck,
destined for a front yard workshop
and a future as his speedy chariot
for going to games,
out with his friends
and to church—
to sing in the choir
with his girlfriend—
when he gets one.

Hope is Finding

Please write or illustrate below what this poem means to you.

*Share your insights with our community by posting them to this poem's web page at <u>**www.Hope-and-Joy.com**</u>*

Hope is Finding

Hope is finding
enough vegetables in the fridge
to feed the family
until the next paycheck comes.

Using white cotton thread
To reinforce seams and patches
in "Goodwill" pants and blouses,
so the rent can be paid.

Taking an aspirin,
when palpitations and discomfort
meet social security and the food supply.

Lighting candles on dark nights,
when the power fails
and rain falls torrentially.

Hope is a sunlight morning
after days and days
of rain and grey clouds.

Hope is Hearing

Please write or illustrate below what this poem means to you.

Share your insights with our community by posting them to this poem's web page at **www.Hope-and-Joy.com**

Hope is Hearing

Hope is hearing
your own heartbeat
late at night,
when your day is over
and the night intrudes,
bringing loneliness
and concentration
on what you don't have
and what you need
not for yourself,
but for your kids' survival.

Hope is finding a solution
to a life of anguish and pain.

Hope is carrying-on.

Hope is The Beginning
of A New Week

Please write or illustrate below what this poem means to you.

Share your insights with our community by posting them to this poem's web page at www.Hope-and-Joy.com

Hope is The Beginning of A New Week

Hope is the beginning of a new week,
when you can clear your mind
of dream-cast demons
and move decisively
from your own troubles
to helping others emerge from theirs.

Hope is the urge you supply
to get things going.
Moving to a new apartment,
changing jobs,
finding a new friend,
beginning a new book,
or writing a letter
to a relative or friend
you haven't spoken to
in a very long time,
but who you thought of
and wanted to renew your relationship.

Hope is receiving that letter.

Hope is A One-Pound Loss

Please write or illustrate below what this poem means to you.

Share your insights with our community by posting them to this poem's web page at www.Hope-and-Joy.com

Hope is A One-Pound Loss

Hope is a one-pound loss
on the first day
of a new diet.

Hope is A Smile

Please write or illustrate below what this poem means to you.

Share your insights with our community by posting them to this poem's web page at www.Hope-and-Joy.com

Hope is A Smile

Hope is a smile
from a co-worker,
for a job you did,
because that's your job,
and you do it every day.

Hope is A Turtle

Please write or illustrate below what this poem means to you.

Share your insights with our community by posting them to this poem's web page at __www.Hope-and-Joy.com__

Hope is A Turtle

Hope is a turtle
finally getting across a very busy street
in the heat of a June day.

It's the reassuring brush
of a chocolate Lab
against the leg of a person
living in a world
of darkness and silence.

It's the rush of children
from a classroom
on the very last day
of the school year—
and the rush to a teacher's face—
when one student leaves
and says, "Thank you!"

Hope is The Very First Cry

Please write or illustrate below what this poem means to you.

Share your insights with our community by posting them to this poem's web page at www.Hope-and-Joy.com

Hope is The Very First Cry

Hope is the very first cry
of a newborn baby
leaving the womb
of its mother.

It's the relief of parents
and doctor,
when all neonatal tests come back
and say,
"Your baby is healthy and normal."

Hope is receiving the deed
to a piece of land
on which you want to build a dream.
It's the words of your builder or realtor,
when he shakes your hand and says,
"Here's the keys to your new home!"
and you use the key
and it works.

Hope is your first step
after your cast comes off—
your second
and third—
until you can run,
feeling the wind
dry your tears of pain.

Hope is Pollen

Please write or illustrate below what this poem means to you.

Share your insights with our community by posting them to this poem's web page at ___www.Hope-and-Joy.com___

Hope is Pollen

Hope is pollen
left in a flower
on a bright sunny day
after rain
has nourished dry soil
and a honeybee
has made its deposit
after a short visit.

Hope is the sweat
rolling down
a farmer's face
after planting
rows and rows
of seeds
under a clear May sun,
after all danger
of frost
is gone
and all the crows
have been scared
away.

Hope is A Bloodworm

Please write or illustrate below what this poem means to you.

Share your insights with our community by posting them to this poem's web page at www.Hope-and-Joy.com

Hope is a Bloodworm

Hope is a bloodworm
wriggling
on the small hook
of a grandchild,
sitting beside her grandpa,
their legs dangling
over a swiftly flowing creek,
their strings floating
on the glistening surface,
his hand
on her shoulder,
his dreams for her…
tucked proudly
in his heart.

Hope is The First Step Forward

Please write or illustrate below what this poem means to you.

Share your insights with our community by posting them to this poem's web page at ***www.Hope-and-Joy.com***

Hope is The First Step Forward

Hope is the first step forward
after two steps back.

Beginning again
after failing,
marshals the whole of your being
toward even the most menial of tasks.

Since failure is the absence of hope,
it takes resolve
and movement
to step forward
and reclaim the energy
you lost
into the black hole of space.

Risking failure's all too common presence,
you take a deep breath
and move ahead,
dismissing all the bumps lying
in the road ahead,
even though you know they are still there.

Hope is The Final Equal

Please write or illustrate below what this poem means to you.

Share your insights with our community by posting them to this poem's web page at www.Hope-and-Joy.com

Hope is The Final Equal

Hope is the final equal
in the calculation
of any formula
for a new product,
service,
plan,
investment,
friendship,
or life.

Hope is Sitting

Please write or illustrate below what this poem means to you.

Share your insights with our community by posting them to this poem's web page at www.Hope-and-Joy.com

Hope is Sitting

Hope is sitting
in a hospital emergency room
waiting for a nurse or doctor
to come to you
with a smile or glimmer
of a self-satisfied feeling
that they have done well
and you should be assured
or content
or happy
with their message.

Medical practitioners want
to feel happy or content
with their mission,
when facing overwhelming burdens
of life threatening injuries and illnesses,
day in and day out.
For them a breath,
a heartbeat,
or a smile
brings hope
and gives them strength
to face their problems
and to give families
and patients hope.

Hope is Finding Affordable Health Insurance

Please write or illustrate below what this poem means to you.

*Share your insights with our community by posting them to this poem's web page at **www.Hope-and-Joy.com***

Hope is Finding Affordable Health Insurance

Hope is finding affordable health insurance
That will pay your bills
When you are no longer employed
and you or your family
are in poor health.

Hope is your health insurer
covering all your healthcare bills,
so your tears flow for the one who is ill
And not the shame of helplessness.

Hope is The Sound

Please write or illustrate below what this poem means to you.

Share your insights with our community by posting them to this poem's web page at __www.Hope-and-Joy.com__

Hope is The Sound

Hope is the sound
of the "crack" of a bat
in a Triple "A" league game
at a friendly
farm community stadium,
where local merchants
not only advertise
on the back boards
of the stadium,
but feed and clothe
the ball players,
giving them a day job
to have some money
in their pockets.

Hope is watching them play
and seeing
a future
"Babe"
"Mickey"
"Sandy"
Or "Willie".

Hope is being called up
to the "Big Leagues"
to show your stuff
…and making it.

Hope is a ball player's wife
packing up
for the eighth time.

Hope is Volunteers

Please write or illustrate below what this poem means to you.

Share your insights with our community by posting them to this poem's web page at www.Hope-and-Joy.com

Hope is Volunteers

Hope is volunteers
and celebrities
working together
to raise money
for little kids
so they can walk,
talk, see or hear.
like other children
who don't need
fundraisers.

Hope is doctors
and scientists
using that money
to find a cure
or at least
a way to ease pain
or make life more livable.

Hope is a child
walking talking,
seeing, or hearing
after a serious battle
with illness or injury.
A smile slowly blooming
across their face,
as they work with determination
and your help
to overcome fear and pain.

Hope is the tears
leaking
from parents' eyes
into creases of joy
no longer hidden
behind smiles of support.

Hope is The Dreams

Please write or illustrate below what this poem means to you.

Share your insights with our community by posting them to this poem's web page at www.Hope-and-Joy.com

Hope is The Dreams

Hope is that the dreams
that wake you up
in the middle of the night
are not real
and won't be remembered
by the time
you find a book of dream symbols
or talk to your best friend about them
over a steaming cup of coffee
and a Krispy Kreme,
while she clucks her tongue
knowingly…or not.

Hope is that when you get
back to sleep
your bad dream
doesn't repeat
or begin where it left off.
Hope is that the Tums work.

Hope is
Nestled In A Dry Place

Please write or illustrate below what this poem means to you.

Share your insights with our community by posting them to this poem's web page at ***www.Hope-and-Joy.com***

Hope is Nestled In A Dry Place

Hope is nestled in
a dry place. Where you
rest your head
amid the steamy moisture
left from the uncatalogued sweat
of dreams you visited
and from which your night
has been delivered.

Hope is waking
with no memory of night dreams,
but just the thrill
of feeling rested
for the beginning
of a new day.

Hope is beginning a new night
at peace with the world
with the lingering softness of a smile
and a goodnight kiss—
in fact,
in memory, or
in anticipation of the night,
from which
future memories will be made.

Hope is The Thin Grey Light

Please write or illustrate below what this poem means to you.

Share your insights with our community by posting them to this poem's web page at www.Hope-and-Joy.com

Hope is The Thin Grey Light

Hope is the thin grey light
as day breaks
after a stormy night.
Large beads of water
and resin
dripping languidly
from summer drenched trees.
Evergreen needles
drooping down,
their veins pumping
with ground water
in plantings
near the floodplain.

Hope is the first rays
of orange sun
piercing somber,
white stuffed clouds,
followed by patches
of blue skies,
fleetingly revealed
as swift storm-fed currents
of fog drift past
to be vaporized
by warm daytime temperatures—
while viewed by early-risers,
can't-sleepers
and night-shifters
finally on their way
home.

Hope is Waking

Please write or illustrate below what this poem means to you.

Share your insights with our community by posting them to this poem's web page at ___www.Hope-and-Joy.com___

Hope is Waking

Hope is waking
to a stuffed nose
and taking an antihistamine
to clear your head
so you can go
back to sleep.

Hope is sleeping
just enough
not to need a nap
in the morning
or to yawn in the middle
of your waking thoughts.

Hope is shutting out
all but the first chirps
of early birds
from your lethargic thoughts,
as you move with increasing determination—
back to bed
and back to sleep
for just 10 more minutes,
just an hour,
just a power nap,
or
perhaps
a power sleep.

Hope is Finding
A Comfortable Place

Please write or illustrate below what this poem means to you.

Share your insights with our community by posting them to this poem's web page at ___www.Hope-and-Joy.com___

Hope is Finding
A Comfortable Place

Hope is finding a comfortable place
to sit, stand, or lean,
when you get up
in the middle of the night
because you ate too much, or
your shoulder or leg hurts—
or you were a jerk the night before,
and you can't enjoy your sleep—
the pain from a limb
or your conscience
annoying you terribly.

Hope is the relief
of confession,
apology,
antacids,
walking back and forth,
or getting a breath of
fresh, cool, night air,
so you can be rid of anxiety,
before the dark
oppressive night
fades to day…
behind silver
moonlight pines…
or your own consolation.

Hope is The First Chirps

Please write or illustrate below what this poem means to you.

Share your insights with our community by posting them to this poem's web page at **www.Hope-and-Joy.com**

Hope is The First Chirps

Hope is the first chirps
of the first bird
to greet the morning
saying, "A new day is here",
"Start again",
"Seek forgiveness",
"You are forgiven",
"Feel better",
"It's ok",
"Go for it" or
"Try again!"
Lots of meanings
for a single, undefined sound,
but an answer
to your dreams.

Hope is Signs

Please write or illustrate below what this poem means to you.

*Share your insights with our community by posting them to this poem's web page at **www.Hope-and-Joy.com***

56

Hope is Signs

Hope is signs
and meanings
that redefine
the road of life...
like Barbasol billboards
on a rural road,
whose age
and time
have long gone by.
Even where they are not seen,
They become beacons
to travelers
who begin to understand
the wisdom
years provide
along an uncharted way.

Hope is Two Beams of Light

Please write or illustrate below what this poem means to you.

*Share your insights with our community by posting them to this poem's web page at **www.Hope-and-Joy.com***

Hope is Two Beams of Light

Hope is two beams of light
moving before you,
to guide you
on a sullen night;
as you move cautiously
along back roads
where clouds hide the moon
and anxiety hides direction.

Hope is Sitting In My Car

Please write or illustrate below what this poem means to you.

*Share your insights with our community by posting them to
this poem's web page at www.Hope-and-Joy.com*

Hope is Sitting In My Car

Hope is sitting in my car
in the middle
of a constant rainstorm
on a busy downtown street
soaking wet—
after trying to fix
windshield wipers
that stopped suddenly
after I left
the relative dryness
of a parking garage.

Hope is having roadside assistance,
getting them on the phone
and after several forays into the deluge,
their telling me
they will tow me
to my dealer
and then I should get a cab home
and it will all be covered
by my auto warranty.

Hope is drying out
while I wait an hour
until a huge tow truck
pulls alongside
and the driver says,
"Hop on board, I am taking you home."

Hope is having someone
Who will answer my call.

Hope is An Angel

Please write or illustrate below what this poem means to you.

Share your insights with our community by posting them to this poem's web page at www.Hope-and-Joy.com

Hope is An Angel

Hope is an angel
nodding
in your direction
at the end
of a prayer.

Hope is Being Prepared

Please write or illustrate below what this poem means to you.

Share your insights with our community by posting them to this poem's web page at __www.Hope-and-Joy.com__

Hope is Being Prepared

Hope is being prepared
for bad weather
and for when
things don't work out
as they should.

Hope is when you need
someone to be there,
to hold your hand,
or listen as you
pour out your heart.

Hope is a strong constitution
and an equally strong faith
in people.
Even though people
aren't always reliable
or helpful.

Hope is when
you need someone,
they are there for you
because
this is the time
you need them to be.

Hope is that
the rain will end
and the sun
will come out,
and the car will start again—
and your life will, too.

Hope is that
grey clouds
become blue skies.

Hope is
Seeing Friendly Faces

Please write or illustrate below what this poem means to you.

*Share your insights with our community by posting them to this poem's web page at **www.Hope-and-Joy.com***

Hope is Seeing Friendly Faces

Hope is seeing friendly faces
in places you used to frequent,
but have been separated from
by time and circumstance.
Hope is seeing that
they recognize you
with fondness
and with a surprised,
but positive expression.

Hope is remembering
their names,
and how you knew them,
and especially
how you left them,
when the space
between you
expanded
and time
crept by.

Hope is renewing
old acquaintances
and creating
new opportunities
to be friends again.
Nurturing
those friendships,
until names
of old friends,
are second nature,
and time
and distance
grow shorter
between you
once again.

Hope is A Grade

Please write or illustrate below what this poem means to you.

Share your insights with our community by posting them to this poem's web page at ***www.Hope-and-Joy.com***

Hope is A Grade

Hope is a grade
on a test
for a kid
who can go somewhere
if he has a key,
a boost,
moral support,
or at least
his parents
and his best friend.

Hope is a pat
on the back
by a coach,
or boss, or mentor,
who doesn't know right then,
but somewhere
down the line
when a decision
is made,
it was the push
in the right direction
with just enough weight
to unbalance the scales
of life
from indecision
to positive action.

Hope is a letter
of recommendation
that may open a door
to a path
that leads unexpectedly
to happiness,
leaving depression
on the back side
of a swinging door.

Hope is A Chance Encounter

Please write or illustrate below what this poem means to you.

Share your insights with our community by posting them to this poem's web page at **www.Hope-and-Joy.com**

Hope is A Chance Encounter

Hope is a chance encounter
with someone
who makes you think;
not about
the ordinary problems
you
or the world
have every day,
but the questions
whose answers
you have always
taken for granted.

Hope is the thought
that suddenly
makes complete sense
and leads you
to solve a puzzle
in a deeply satisfying way.

Hope is A Step

Please write or illustrate below what this poem means to you.

Share your insights with our community by posting them to this poem's web page at www.Hope-and-Joy.com

Hope is A Step

Hope is a step
in the right direction
on a thin
and rocky trail
in woods
so dense
you could get lost
and never be found
again.

Hope is an inspiration
in street clothes,
no angel wings,
no horoscope,
just common wisdom
that makes you think
and be
what you really can.

Hope is A Surprise

Please write or illustrate below what this poem means to you.

Share your insights with our community by posting them to this poem's web page at **www.Hope-and-Joy.com**

Hope is A Surprise

Hope is a surprise
birthday party
with your friends,
reminding you
that life
is not made up of clocks
insidiously ticking-away
your infinity,
but of people
who identify
with even just
a single thing you do
and memories
of what you did,
as well as glimpses
of what could be.

Hope is A Sermon

Please write or illustrate below what this poem means to you.

Share your insights with our community by posting them to this poem's web page at www.Hope-and-Joy.com

Hope is A Sermon

Hope is a sermon,
a lecture,
a line in a story,
a science experiment
that works;
a pleasure designed
from the measures
of your life.

Hope is a trip
among the stars,
when you are only planning
a visit down a tired lane.

Hope is A Wish

Please write or illustrate below what this poem means to you.

*Share your insights with our community by posting them to this poem's web page at **www.Hope-and-Joy.com***

Hope is A Wish

Hope is a wish
for a happy birthday—
a reminder
that you are alive
and able
to face another day
in a new year,
no matter when.

Hope is a clear signal
of the start of something
you have never done before,
no matter how many times
you have done it.

Hope is The Beginning

Please write or illustrate below what this poem means to you.

Share your insights with our community by posting them to this poem's web page at ***www.Hope-and-Joy.com***

Hope is The Beginning

Hope is the beginning
of a new day,
sleep gluing your eyelids closed
against the new sun,
anxiety pulling at each muscle,
anticipation splashing cold water
on the old year's dreams,
determination,
brewing fresh hot coffee
to wake up
your taste buds,
so you can take
a bite out of the challenges
the new day will bring.

Hope is
A Carpenter's Hammer

Please write or illustrate below what this poem means to you.

*Share your insights with our community by posting them to this poem's web page at **www.Hope-and-Joy.com***

Hope is A Carpenter's Hammer

Hope is a carpenter's hammer
nailing boards together
to frame a new room
or a new house.

Hope is choosing
the colors for the baby's room,
buying a cradle,
putting away a few dollars
for a grandchild's education.

Hope is bringing
a loaf of bread,
a box of salt,
and a bouquet of fresh flowers
to a child's first apartment
or home,
when they move out
of your home
and move in
to a new life
on their own.

Hope is Visiting

Please write or illustrate below what this poem means to you.

Share your insights with our community by posting them to this poem's web page at www.Hope-and-Joy.com

Hope is Visiting

Hope is visiting
With a new neighbor,
making a new friend.

Hope is talking till dawn
with someone
you've just met.

Hope is meeting someone
you haven't seen
for a long, long time.

Hope is a new beginning.

Hope is The Ache

Please write or illustrate below what this poem means to you.

Share your insights with our community by posting them to this poem's web page at www.Hope-and-Joy.com

Hope is The Ache

Hope is the ache
in your legs
pumping
up and down
in place
to the pace
of a choreographed tape.
Each step
a reminder
of how much
you are no longer
in shape,
and how portions
of your flesh
drape
over a no longer
youthful frame.

Hope is knowing
It is yourself you blame.
An indifferent youth,
hiding from the truth,
that age is not an excuse
for growing bigger
and forgetting—
just because it tastes good.

The results of a lifetime
of eating foods
that provided solace--early-on,
are pounds
that resist pounding
of late.

Hope is building your
Body... again.

Hope is The Joy

Please write or illustrate below what this poem means to you.

*Share your insights with our community by posting them to this poem's web page at <u>**www.Hope-and-Joy.com**</u>*

Hope is The Joy

Hope is the joy
on the teary-eyed faces
of mothers and fathers
standing in their "Sunday-best"
as their sons and daughters
stand in love, awe, and fear
of what they are getting into.

Hope is entering the wedding ceremony,
bride's arm in yours,
looking at the faces of friends and family.
Seeing their reflected joy--
their hope for your children--
as they face the future together.

Hope is the look in each of their eyes—
children and parents—
as they prepare for an adventure
neither have experienced,
but both have thought about
from the moment
they knew each other
and thought there might be a chance
for a forever together.

Hope Flourishes

Please write or illustrate below what this poem means to you.

Share your insights with our community by posting them to this poem's web page at __www.Hope-and-Joy.com__

Hope Flourishes

Hope flourishes
When pouring flavors
of friendship
into bowls of
love, honesty and respect.

Hope is A Spirited Step

Please write or illustrate below what this poem means to you.

Share your insights with our community by posting them to this poem's web page at ***www.Hope-and-Joy.com***

Hope is A Spirited Step

Hope is a spirited step
down a yellow brick road
lined with roses and thorns,
goblins and angels.

Hope is The Light

Please write or illustrate below what this poem means to you.

Share your insights with our community by posting them to this poem's web page at ***www.Hope-and-Joy.com***

Hope is The Light

Hope is the light
each generation shares
with the generations gone before
and generations to come.

Hope is the dream
of our ancestors
and the fulfillment
of our descendants.

Hope is tomorrow,
even as we awaken
today.

Hope is A Fine Strong Line

Please write or illustrate below what this poem means to you.

Share your insights with our community by posting them to this poem's web page at www.Hope-and-Joy.com

Hope is A Fine Strong Line

Hope is a fine strong line
holding tightly together
those who begin
a project or cause
to those who toil
to complete it
and to those who
benefit from its completion.

Hope is a connection
from idea
to implementation,
from beginning
to end,
from life givers
to life savers.

Hope is a line
to mend
wounds and fences
and to bind users
to providers.

Hope is a line
that weaves us
together.

Hope is The Net

Please write or illustrate below what this poem means to you.

*Share your insights with our community by posting them to this poem's web page at **www.Hope-and-Joy.com***

Hope is The Net

Hope is the net
designed by a succession
of weavers,
one hand at a time
over and under,
in and out.
Made of different colors
and different materials,
each strand
reinforcing the other.

Hope is in the strength
The loops and ropes
create, surrounding the burden
they are built to carry.
A myriad of holes
bound together,
their strength
only as one whole net
not each weave.

Hope is the strength
each user
takes for granted
and the weaver's fingers
imbue in their work.

Hope is The Drying of Tear Drops

Please write or illustrate below what this poem means to you.

Share your insights with our community by posting them to this poem's web page at **www.Hope-and-Joy.com**

Hope is The Drying of Tear Drops

Hope is the drying
of tear drops
from eyes wet
with sorrow,
washed by pain.

Hope is sobbing,
muffled by arms
encircling a body
patting reassurance,
soothing
ruffled feelings
and rumpled hair.

Day turns into night,
And night to day.
Searing dread
diminishes
in sunlight's exposure
of shadows and edges.

Hope renews the spirit,
once again.

Hope is The Chirp

Please write or illustrate below what this poem means to you.

*Share your insights with our community by posting them to this poem's web page at **www.Hope-and-Joy.com***

Hope is The Chirp

Hope is the chirp
of a lone bird
that you hear
after a night of anguish.

Pictures of nightmares
slowly erase
from your closed eyelids
and runaway fears.

Hope breaks through with daybreak
and you realize
you can start again.
Take a step, now
in the direction
of tomorrow.

Hope is an open door
at the gate
for an airplane
to a familiar destination.

Hope is Waiting

Please write or illustrate below what this poem means to you.

Share your insights with our community by posting them to this poem's web page at __www.Hope-and-Joy.com__

Hope is Waiting

Hope is waiting
to see an old friend,
anticipating
what he or she will say
when seeing you again,
after a long absence,
when so much has happened
between you
and them,
and those they confided in
about you.

Joy is finally seeing them alone,
or as only one in a crowd.
Joy is when
their first words
are the words your heart
is waiting to hear—
no matter what their first words are.

A
BOOK
of
JOY

Joy is A Child's Smile

Please write or illustrate below what this poem means to you.

Share your insights with our community by posting them to this poem's web page at ***www.Hope-and-Joy.com***

Joy is A Child's Smile

Joy is a child's smile
at a parent's touch.
A husband's glance at
his wife of any years,
when in confidence
he says or does something
he knows she will understand,
whether it is out of desperation
or inspiration.

Joy is a couple's willingness
to trust each other
and their reward for thinking
and doing alike.

Joy is a symphony
played by an orchestra
after weeks of practice
to its audience's delight…
and the conductor's relief.

Joy fills a heart
pounding with anticipation,
when all or any expectations
are fulfilled.

Joy is Descending Into Cool Depths

Please write or illustrate below what this poem means to you.

Share your insights with our community by posting them to this poem's web page at www.Hope-and-Joy.com

Joy is Descending Into Cool Depths

Joy is descending
into the cool depths
of a clear swimming pool
on a warm, sultry day;
cares and distractions
sloughing off into the
cleansing waters,
evaporating into the warm
humid air about you.

Joy is re-experiencing
the pre-natal feeling of
life's fluids in a mother's womb.
Immersed in her gel-like pool,
thriving in her soothing atmosphere,
moving in tune with her sensual rhythms.
Engaged with the circles of waves
radiating from each movement.

Joy is not counting
the ripples, but
savoring that you
are able to appreciate
making the ripples
in your own pool of life.

Joy is Food

Please write or illustrate below what this poem means to you.

Share your insights with our community by posting them to this poem's web page at __www.Hope-and-Joy.com__

Joy is Food

Joy is eating
food another has
prepared,
experiencing the taste
and texture of their
preparation,
the sense and care
of their planning,
the sensuality of how
their fingers plied
and kneaded the bread,
caressed the fruit
and coaxed love
from nature
for you.

Joy is Experiencing Passion

Please write or illustrate below what this poem means to you.

Share your insights with our community by posting them to this poem's web page at www.Hope-and-Joy.com

Joy is Experiencing Passion

Joy is experiencing passion
for whatever you do in life,
from the least exhilarating,
to the most fraught with trepidation.

Joy is creating passion
in others and knowing
without saying,
you were the author of their joy.

Joy is hearing others exclaim that
they have seen what you in your
joy have revealed to them.

Joy is the coinciding
of directions you are given
and the routes you discover.

Joy is living each day,
understanding what a privilege
you have
to be allowed to
discover your own route—
from the time you awake
to the time you choose to sleep.

Joy is Getting Up In the Morning

Please write or illustrate below what this poem means to you.

Share your insights with our community by posting them to this poem's web page at ___*www.Hope-and-Joy.com*___

Joy is Getting Up In the Morning

Joy is getting up in the morning
and getting out of bed.
A new day.
The sun rising without a cloud
and the previous
night's storm gone.
Sweet bird songs replacing
horrific claps of thunder
amid slashes of white lightning and
the constant staccato of hail.

Joy is a beautiful new day
and the spark
of new adventures
each fresh moment brings.

Joy is Growth

Please write or illustrate below what this poem means to you.

Share your insights with our community by posting them to this poem's web page at **www.Hope-and-Joy.com**

Joy is Growth

Joy is finding people
who are honestly interested in you.
Not just because they profit from you,
but because
you, through them,
can profit even more.

Your profit is
your return on your investment.
Their profit is your personal growth.

In the end,
the sum of all profits
is the relationships you build and
how you continue to grow together.

Joy is both of you,
doing what is best for each other;
that is true growth.

Joy is Knowledge

Please write or illustrate below what this poem means to you.

Share your insights with our community by posting them to this poem's web page at www.Hope-and-Joy.com

Joy is Knowledge

Joy is knowledge,
not only in the mind of the beholder,
but in your mind
and his or her touch, taste, hearing or sight.

Joy is experiencing
all that artwork conveys and
all the response artwork evokes.

Joy is making art
part of your life and being
and acquiring art
for the places you live
and for your life, itself.

Joy is Sunny Days

Please write or illustrate below what this poem means to you.

Share your insights with our community by posting them to this poem's web page at <u>***www.Hope-and-Joy.com***</u>

Joy is Sunny Days

Joy is
sunny days,
cool nights,
soothing rain showers,
and
soft quiet blankets of snow.

They make you smile
when you are dressed for them,
and protected from the wet and cold.

They make you feel nature responding
all around you,
welcoming
each new generation to life.

Joy is when crocus and daffodil
break the surface of winter's frost
to bloom in cold morning mists,
among fresh blades of grass.
announcing nature's call
for new life to welcome
the first days
of a changing season.

Joy is the Cry of a New Born Baby

Please write or illustrate below what this poem means to you.

*Share your insights with our community by posting them to this poem's web page at **www.Hope-and-Joy.com***

Joy is the Cry of a New Born Baby

Joy is the cry of a new born baby
as it slips
from the comforting
confines of its mother's
womb into the
encyclopedia of life and
the thesaurus of life's experiences.

Joy is the changes each day
and each week brings,
as a new baby grows
into a smile, a laugh,
a bubbling sound.
As it makes its own
terms with the environment
into which it is born.

Joy Is The Freedom To Dance

Please write or illustrate below what this poem means to you.

Share your insights with our community by posting them to this poem's web page at **www.Hope-and-Joy.com**

Joy Is The Freedom To Dance

Joy is the freedom to dance
a Chadash or a Polka.
Not worrying
if the music is too loud,
or will disturb
the unkind majority,
or lead to rocks, sticks or bullets
and the hangman's noose
to end the party.

Joy is breathing easily and clearly
in the morning's dreary breeze
after celebrating
an Italian, Jewish, Polish,
Hindi, African or Muslim wedding…
in a free country.

Joy is crying tears of happiness
over a celebration of love,
in a land where you are free to celebrate
without fearing
that no sun will come out
on the morrow.

Joy is the answer to the prayer of love.
Amen.

Joy Is The Warmth Of
A Baby's Head

Please write or illustrate below what this poem means to you.

Share your insights with our community by posting them to this poem's web page at www.Hope-and-Joy.com

Joy Is The Warmth Of A Baby's Head

Joy is the warmth
of a baby's head,
nestled against my cheek.
A smile blossoming,
after I tickle her
chin with my index finger.

Her tug at my shoulder
as she clutches my shirt
to hold herself
just slightly above the
burp cloth her
mother laid down,
so my silk shirt shouldn't bear
the stains of a milky dinner.

Joy is clutching the future
to my bosom,
feeling tomorrow grow.

Joy is Living in God's Plan

Please write or illustrate below what this poem means to you.

Share your insights with our community by posting them to this poem's web page at **www.Hope-and-Joy.com**

Joy is Living in God's Plan

Joy is living in God's plan,
even if you don't believe in God.

Seeing and hearing
what is revealed
each moment
you live through.
Living each moment,
as if not another moment
will arise.

Joy is knowing
living your life
fully is your joy.

Joy is Sitting in a Quiet Place

Please write or illustrate below what this poem means to you.

Share your insights with our community by posting them to this poem's web page at ***www.Hope-and-Joy.com***

Joy is Sitting in A Quiet Place

Joy is sitting in a quiet place.
Staring at a lowering sun
and a rising moon;
knowing that in the moment
before sunset, all the earth
is waiting
for the rewinding
of the day's clock,
the flush of two lovers' cheeks
and the lingering kiss
of night and day.

Joy is Finishing a Marathon

Please write or illustrate below what this poem means to you.

Share your insights with our community by posting them to this poem's web page at ___www.Hope-and-Joy.com___

Joy is Finishing a Marathon

Joy is finishing a marathon.
Breathing the heavy perfume
of labor's sweat.
Luxuriating in the warm
bath of excitement,
a significant
accomplishment brings.

Joy is knowing
you are right,
even when no one acknowledges
your contribution.

Joy is seeing your ideas and dreams
come true.

Joy is a poor man's face
brightening
when his cup
is full;
even though he never
heard or felt it filling.

About the Author

Ronald Harvey Wohl is an observer of life in all its forms and an optimist in his views. He has been writing poetry since he was twelve. He has always had a strong interest in people: how they react to what life does to them, how they affect each other and how they communicate with each other. He is an applied psychological anthropologist, Certified Management Consultant, civic activist, politician, businessman and mentor. He is president of In Plain English®, a management communication consulting firm and vice president of his wife's firm, Wohl Communication Services, Inc. He was chair of the Montgomery County, Maryland Commission on the Humanities. He is a member of the board of directors of the Plain Language Association InterNational (PLAIN), promoting the use of plain language worldwide. And was a member of the national board of directors of the Institute of Management Consulting. He is a speaker and author on communication and management topics.

He is married to his college sweetheart, Myrna Chevelier Wohl, for over 49 years. His two daughters, Jennifer and Amy, husbands Mark and Steve, and grandchildren Anabelle, Henry and Nathan bring him his greatest pleasure and education.